Sonnetailia

Sonnetailia

Marc Nasdor

ROOF BOOKS
NEW YORK

ISBN: 978-1-931824-27-9
Library of Congress Catalog Card Number: 2007938818
Cover art by Hieronymus Bosch, "The Garden of Earthly Delights" (detail)
Author photo by Bálint Fülöp

For my son, Emil

and in memory of Hugues de la Plaza (1970-2007)

Sections of *Sonnetailia* have appeared in the following magazines and journals, online and print: *Talisman, The Brooklyn Rail, Jacket, Perfect 8* and *level: socially conscious poetry.*

This book owes thanks to many for its existence, notably Anne Tardos and the late Jackson Mac Low for lovingly pestering me during a 14-year period of inactivity. Deep appreciation to, among others, Anikó Bognár, András Böröcz, Steve Cannon, Alan Davies, Mónica de la Torre, Richard Ellsberry, John Ellsberry, Ed Foster, Sharon Mesmer, Charlie Morrow, Nobuho Nagasawa, Ruth Nasdor, Murat Nemet-Nejat, Doug Retzler, Robbin Ami Silverberg, Christy Singleton, Vlada Tomova and Elizabeth Vahlsing for their continual support of my work.

Special thanks to M.W., without whom this book would never have been completed.

Roof Books are distributed by
Small Press Distribution
1341 Seventh Avenue
Berkeley, CA. 94710-1403
Phone orders: 800-869-7553
www.spdbooks.org

This book was made possible, in part, with public funds from the New York State Council on the Arts, a state agency.

Roof Books are published by
Segue Foundation
300 Bowery
New York, NY 10012
seguefoundation.com

Contents

I.

Detached for Analysis

1/1: A nightmare on M Street

Pocket annotation to the Black Hole of Calcutta (JPEGs
of Guantanamo real estate) with knights and bishops
drenched in a septic tongue-kiss. Custodians of the match
stand: mopping-up of a half-gallon of bloody quarters
tossed about the amphitheater, hollering *pardon us
into your wits, O Fifth Columnist of Sixteen drawn off
in the distance abreast of the cathedral.* June firebreath
and a quiet interregnum for us to get lashed across
the ass. *Amass, amass!* Here how seasons and pieces
aggregate: these moves may continue until the snow
gets plowed (at least) but at best a draw. This year
in shots of the prison revolt, we'll be conscious of who
crossed the room, who brown-nosed their way between
this world and the last, and where have we gone
to return to a state
                    in such a state, buckets
overhead and forward: March.

1/2: The hunchback of aspartame

Death excitement culminates broadly and timed to clash
with events. *What about epidemics?* The rich hallucinate
a famine in their midst (tonal violence via medieval
technology via evidence of civil undernourishment);
a balanced week of social coercion and supernatural
activities clustered. Trial by disaster footage—mouth-
to-mouth insinuations erect—extended to dependents
through power-of-attorney. But faint spiritual land-
marks diminish via poltergeists attached to the fringe:
not a shred of belief, awareness of number, bishopric
sensitivity to a world of demons even cuter than
the multitudes. [There] where only space the tormentable
troubled earth. April in Paris. Gargoyles pressed
into descriptions to be disseminated, peacefully above
the human traffic of marvels
                        repossessed;
tender carvings photocopied overnight.

1/3: Super Bowl halftime circumcision

Avenue around, my back on bottom to remind you. Switch
this room with a slaughter pen, *then what?* My hand said
"dent" and afterwards only smoke and right after that
see telephone in toilet. Here (as here) as mean element
transport. Offsides and out: holding, pushing. *Blow
red bird light*, plunked down hard out the wheedling
mendicant's pantslegs, airhorns pivoting forth
toward the tassels, peckerwood suicide in the leggings
of his hausfrau. *Not now.* Throwing that, and everything
that looks like that, to the free world traders. Bombs
and badges, conk the campers, another bobo with a corn
in his worm; but where the millions clucking at the doors
to their vaults? And whose hand wrapped in a horsewhip
projected into the alcove ascribed to? Earnest counter-
weight steady for use

                in presenting apparitions
out of bistro intestinal sawdust.

1/4: End Times in the restroom

They are frightened of themselves. They allow dogfish
into their temples, obtain facts through alacrity,
feast on the heads of their dog-god enemies, contract
acute symptoms of Wide Sargasso Trenchmouth, bulltooth
butterballs tabled to spreadsheets. And whose changelings
to compare them to? Yet reasoning for the rest of us.
Skinner of questions and questioners, formation especially
of immoderate representatives defecting. "We can explain
this war dance but not to those who've had their legs
shot off." Here where everyone watches the natives kiss,
a necessary reaction regarding the former. *The citizens
have stopped having intercourse,* and to this end let us
fast; yet others have others made homeless it seems
for contrast. Out to the godless forests—*who says so?*
The trees have reacted

                        to this attitude by expiring,
home to resist and squarely against history.

1/5: Totally consensual sex under duress

Standing too close to the Baba inadvisable. Is it you
or everyone else? Elements pull—rubber / air / magnesium
(rubber?)—four in unison roll across a pressed mineral
surface. Taxi stand. You or both of us in position
at the poop curb: figure in undershirt, quarter-hour block
to entrance onto throughway, squares that drive
and stick; stopped on signal and Disappeared. Now we have
a future with a name on it: *go to prison and stay there.*
Reckless endangerment, negligent homicide, weekends
off for conjugal Visitation, walking walking walking trot.
Closer to the harbor no vehicles save jitneys (substance
I'm thought to have taken takes hold). Judge *when*
and *how* and *why.* Substantive weather presumes
phenomena brewing, moving off into "suck-a-dizzy-planet"
waking up in the middle of
                                    currency in general,
small denominations particular.

1/6: Impersonism: a *festschrift*

Function follows the rest, that's why I'm sobbing.
How did I get stuck in the String of Intermissions? Sash
that gets pulled and dropped, or the drawing out
of a big blank thoughtful stink. Exercise the extreme
but perhaps she's only bolted from the cab. Heretofore
alone myself, remaining functions extended to infinity,
lost horizontals of earth or water merely to circle and
circle. Assuming "please" won't help, all sixteen weathered
benevolents tarpaulin'd down for the summer tsunamis.
Then off it peals, blended into obscurantism alas at least
aghast for him and his *doppelschmutz;* soap bubbles truck-
loaded from eardrumming engines and the beings inside
treadmilling like sex gerbils. Where are they floating off to?
The friends of our enemies' friends are home watching
everything, mistaken

                    for words they'll assume;

exact means "to exact."

1/7: For those about to rock

Heavy blocks thump on the earth; no rolling hills
to run off to. Relief to truly blow it and this time
irrevocably. What color cigars should we buy for it?
Which nationality the coachman's daughter and how
long the barrel of his shotgun? Only imagine *because;*
please define spiteful determination. If this were merely
political we'd have nothing else to worry us. Today a semi-
official rainstorm confiscates the last beautiful morning
I spent between your [somehow] inscrutable gams. No one
feigned surprise or else maybe we thought tomorrow
was Backwards Day but I was amiss; and one shouldn't
forget we're only back in these bodies about a month, *as if.*
Convoluted solstice to be played and rewound if anything
is possible; now to the task of emptying the contents
of my watering can
                    out the window
where a quick summary follows.

1/8: The human genome spank test

Granite slabs up, asphalt slabs over. Oranges in a bowl
plummet southward head to hand. And this is what
you get back from the lab: five bright futures and one
at the end of each. Parboiled pan-fry, Naugahyde plaque
to nativism splashed off. You and the others *(you
and what others?)* More of everything for the effects,
and so long as it sits right with me if I haven't started
bleeding. You and your "wives" mounted at the ends
of your arms. But here in this kingdom, illness
to be your fair cut: long shot of lymph straight down
the umbilical piece—preserving itself to be opened
if coated—your own remedy which comes out of you.
Life purged twice, willfully numerous as sciences left
to the progeny, another reconnoiter in the dark;
honkies anointed in the Diatribe Room,

                                    detached for analysis
and otherwise starved but *case closed.*

1/9: But the chemicals assume otherwise

Lights out, moment of collusion spurs pathetic outcry.
A certain colonial party summons the human go-between
to a spot behind the chapel. He who delivers incendiary
prayers, he who scrubs the dais clean with cock's blood
and organ meat. What have they offered us to make good
of their war-mongering social studies? Get thine Ass
back in church and grind thy scabby, postulating kneecaps
deep into its plush pile carpet. Is there a name given
to the god who once lanced his Great Boil and allowed
your souls to plummet freely to earth? Search and destroy
your luggage; identify each mistake committed herewith.
When you reach your destination you will drop your things
and lower yourselves into the stew; and there below,
at the bottom of the pot, will your gills clog and cause
you to dissipate,
                  color your blood broth-green,
usher you back to your food chain.

1/10: Potty politics

Propane temples determine windows to the left, like
large locks foot by foot on the causeway. A thousand
errant impossibilities, bound as ever as strangers form
into a semicircle, there the esteemed place polluted
according to zeal factor. Furniture of the Lodge,
brothers under the Sign of the Water Buffalo. Here
priests hang from rafters; Emperor Opportunity secures
the ladders of pain, whereupon life rises to the right
and to "liberty." But where then affix the critical lines
that keep the world apace? Where the vacation spot
of the Inestimable Suicide Kingdom? Enter your edifice
by any portal you choose. Inertia yes or inertia no,
I propose melancholy astonishment on the express ramp—
the Whole People—merely a length backwards in inches
and reaction. Proclaim
                    and cut loose;
six padlocks, the fewer the better.

1/11: Backchanneled flat-earth apologia

Mental-case service and poseurs atypical; scholar-kings
in relief on wallboards adjoining. We plaster three
square, roofing in the sun which the coarse buffalo-
grass has grown out from. Siege of force by nature
and warmed-over vestigial obligations of the army;
only fear of pacification except for getting wounded
abroad. And besides resistance, what else is there
until it's through? Will hunger end according to them?
They will offer to seal the enclosures and forget
to inform the inhabitants. Collect and surrender, collect
and surrender; seize the dead and lay into their fortresses.
Resuscitate the napes of their necks and prepare
to accord blame to the next object of humility,
unbound henceforth from its homestead, concluded
and "touched," elbowed
                          at odd angles of those
at peace with their cultures respectively.

1/12: Provocations of the fire-pissing rite

Calling business, greeting credit: these methods worked
well but that was before the lab techs blew their own
nuts off. *Brune* or *Bruin* figure as we knew it (appearance
upon its approach) rifled through our bags, jumped sixty
stories north and landed on the roof—not so unamazing
if you ever met the guy/gal/beast/circuit. Just how many
geniuses can one city put up with? Not enough towers
and an air traffic controller for every seven Buckets
of Whup Ass. At night in the bluish privacy of their powder
rooms, saturnine wood nymphs and goat boys prayed to,
should they deign to reanimate and spring from the wall-
paper. And then to consider the following query, insect
of insects though it appear: is there anything I could execute
to make your life simpler? "Double *nay* or triple *neigh!*"
Last year I got torn to shreds,

                                this year I'm absorbing
my tissues, next year I dissolve to base elements.

1/13: Weed and feed

Gastrointestinal peripherals in a spring-loaded self-
collapsing chassis. Looking around as in front to back
(in the second instance "to a watery grave") but not
this way. Listening—meaning brain-pharynx-mouth-space-
canal-drum-hammer-anvil-stirrup-fluid-brain—balked
before Judgment call. Regarding house, regarding
lawn; beholders of tic fits gyrating off the hoods
of their jeeps, and the medium at the Table of Good
Looks playing litigant for the rest of the séance. These
and others I invited into my bed in the worst manner
possible. Glassy-eyed freshman undertakers petrified
before blank slabs first day on the job. No sirens
or theme music for presentation of work, nor simple
gesture of graceful scalpel against dead meat, blended
with a huge fuss
            of questions to the partner,
having been driven away.

1/14: Dispatches from the precinct

Red pig White pig fatty-Blue-pig: three engaged
in somersault activity bearing Statue of Liberty
complexions to boot. What is being explained across
the diameter of this proof-print? Tight-assed and
cracked of tooth, seemingly malfeasable at ground
level and tied to the trellis, at once concentric
and askew. Bludgeoned by their hatpins; drenched
sticky in his own verisimilitude; painted sloppily about
the inside of his shower stall which looks something
like the inside of his head. Is *that* who it was sitting
next to him with the vise-grip? The shell of his
erstwhile muscular foot; the spot where he turns on
his monitor and pulls in a tidal wave; intersection
of the cosines between home number and work
number at least
                    a quarter length up the alley
and smack into a security gate.

1/15: They are not at the beach

Reflexes ticktock off sundials manufactured *in medias res*
apocalypse-scare. Consecutive summer blisterprints: no
twelve-tone perseverance junkies climbing all over
the hedge. Where have all the nippers gone? Once again so,
embezzled and extorted and giving it all back in order
that it will have been forgotten by the conclusion of this
episode; or the last six pairs of headache and bodyache
prepared and delivered at the tongue-lashing. Yet out
in the neighborhoods the labor of shock troops affixed
to accumulate, nonplussed or entangled in great promise
of peace. Ours meaning everybody's. Heavy ankles of a
predatory public squashed into corpse-plugged fields.
And later on a last layer of dust protected from the wind,
smeared across bony insteps of the twang-throated
skeletons, nervous not in the least
                              and accelerated
through the sleeves of their overcoats.

1/16: The manatees are really, *really* heavy

Bass-reflex. Four million years of human prehistory
to produce *this?* Never in my life have I had to put up
with my own ilk until the moment before; signs and sounds
in bubble-wrapped envelopes dispatched to the tropics.
Where is such a place as where beauty has prolonged
itself for the maiden voyage previously missed? Qualified
maybe as would yield the Supreme Being each first
of the month. *Not* the Man's punching fist in the garbage
can lid, but clock-faced children and regenerated spouses
landing on the shore in great elliptical sailboards of strung-
together bones and piranha-chewed husbands to begin life
as smooth-skinned crocodiles; now and forever on the beach
and up the mountain, pounding away at a rock, ramming
a trapdoor back to civilization—everything here including
computers and tractor-trailers

                    and poisonous bunny rabbits
hopping on the Electric Chair.

II.

Grown Men Evaporating

2/1: One nation [of pedophobes] under God

Something naughty begins a slow contracted course
through the reservoir of his pigpen, dispatches him promptly
to the slammer; and though nothing reflective of his
internecine predilections, all the same to bullwhip chain-gang
and porkpie hats vomited into his soup can, changing
the color of his nubile proboscis to a deepening shade
of goldenrod. Only now there's a leopard up his nose he won't
talk about, a quilt of algae blooming on the lake in which
he'll submerse himself on the anniversary of the morning
his old man blew into space, fuzzy dachshunds nodding
in agreement from the windshields in the back of his head.
But where do his sympathies lie? Who's that whimpering
in his mutagenic crib? A section from the tailpiece
of his toy fighter-bomber dislodges into his throat,
his belated cry for help
                    misheard by millions
of photons plunging into and out of the planet.

2/2: Depreciation sonnet (why it's better to rent)

Hagioscopic angle isolated to force labor east, outfitted
with its own gravediggers to describe and consist,
consist and describe, altogether livid and working
as agents of heroism thereafter discounted. Condensed
in the nerve endings, intensive endeavors and then
quickly to abolish the banks and brokerages, as
now it's our turn to fight the police or *be* the police;
yet next time not to bother handing us the opportunity
to press butt-cheek against glass. Property hoarded
over centuries comes crawling home, only now it's packing
its piece *(of the what?)*—a piece of the *what* in "whatever."
If the circumference of its willpower expands to include
the linked-up cylinders of its vertebrae, *what* then bodes
for the avenging children, chomping away at its column
as it charges across grasslands
                              with backhoe and pickaxe
to recalibrate the space-time continuum.

2/3: Deicide under the mistletoe

Blood memory is an open fist: plenty of time to account
for who owns what and who has to pay for the wash. Hours
consume years in reverse, number-drunk who must slash
into his own sex glands and shun all rooms off behind
the periphery; as when a newborn something, having time
which dries all over it, then snatches the clutch to spin it
out of gear. What the individualist memory wants is
assurance—one square foot of floorspace and a match
to take in the furniture as well. It is the twenty-year cycle
and the principle of displacement in this town: gas
for instance but preferably alcohol, beginning with fixture
evacuation late into the night, returning next morning
to a fresh empty lot; coming to a halt before sociologist's
revolver; shoving *they* hands down deep into *they* pockets
and the airspace between

somebody's boot, several
unidentified objects, and the door.

2/4: Real estate for crabs

Evenings in Baltipest, city that brotherly slurped itself
into existence. From *Mitteleuropa* to Mid-Atlantic geo-
graphical curtailment, longhorns and webfeet will fall
from their transport devices and dance until Doomsday.
(Which day that? Pray and tell.) Cadavers pile up in the city
of my mirth and the village of yours; neckties will stream
out the portals of our buses and trams such that schools of
winnowing horses get slapped in the eyes and bolt roughshod
into traffic, toss off their riders, stagger onto thorough-
fares, twirl on three hooves in the direction of "thataway,"
and sink to gesticulate when the wills of their masters
have crumbled for good. Later on the humans might even find
a name for it, but perhaps the alas-sayers will beat them
to their targets. *(Who's holding whose breath?)* Brackish
waters to flood the haylofts,
                    nostril to nostril
a crustacean with a family to return to.

2/5: Assheads in Humvees

What a whaste! The president and his love pickle might have
blossomed in pinworms and spit up "secular" "humanism."
Only now though he drowns in the other half of history, salt-free
potatoes are what they'll find in his brain, boiled-dry
rice cakes strewn across the floor, and the caretaker inside
mopping up its disgusting lavatory, whipping tile
in a sudsy frenzy like a mad dentist at *his* profession's
equivalent of a firearms social. Which means to specify
the following: upon discovery a continent shrinks back
in denial; kingfishers swerve and spiral in arcs (moon
still visible beneath the horizon). Signal response, signal
response. Bake the earth or leave it as-is. These minor
differences will always irreconcile and therefore as well
the fruits of his labia. Go out and seek a rapport
to eviscerate, conquer and promise
                              reassembly postpartum,
spend and save, deceive repent.

2/6: Parental advisory

Devotional plumber turns reactionary not surprisingly
(off-key, perhaps) but notice what's flaking off the pipes
into the water table. Needless to say to the pinnacle
of his pocket—"oh no I don't, oh no I ain't!" *Muchos
mojitos* to the gas and electric gastro-electable, systems
over phenomena partial towards the future. Whose is
the system I adore, boor? Milliseconds to convert to.
Noseblowing gut-plundering engine-backfiring diddle-
fiddling cheek-pinching *tooth-flossing man-whore!* Straight
through my underthings doth its curious pinky now excavate.
Gong-hammering twig-snapping backflips from bathtub
to bathtub with handfuls of hair grease to make the ride
smarmier. *Ode to Joy, Mr. Elephant Testicles.* Rubber baby
bunko buggery. Treetop toad-sliming all about the house,
come hooked on the fangs

                    of its chortly capital offspring
via superconducting drain-snake comeuppance.

2/7: Imaginary uprising of the adjuncts

Seven is the blocking numeral as explained on the box;
three or four subsequent, betwixt puberty and the ascension
of Holy Terror to the porcelain ejector seat. Slave This
wriggles up the coccyx of Master Heretofore from spine
to spine towards freedom or decay. Which blind mouse wove
itself into the niche at the head of the cryptocracy? Bilious
milieu-producing organisms of occasion barricade the exits
and yell *sleep!* at the offended listenership. Otherwise,
and in addition, the word "whence" may serve as a kind of
heat-exchanger for the overeducated and temporally dismissed.
Not me, I'm holding it in until after my lunch. Me and the Mrs.
walked for hours and neither of us made it as far as the boat
launch; we tried naming names but that only gave us
a headache. In any case, a good night's rest might help
both of us feel better;
                    there's a gallon of effluvium
in the fridge we do not want to know about.

2/8: An eschatology of waterbeds

Trestle miscalculation amounts to jointed metal
arching reptile, reversely tangential as a curve rolling
downward gently from a line connecting here and hereafter.
Twinklers rotund and twinklers rococo shuttle through
strings of a loom between the rocks of a streambed below.
But how do inanimate objects express dread? What kind
of sentence or question cannot mitigate? Everything
rotates yet only the pugilist takes advantage of this.
Tubular wind-chimes warn no one in a vacuum. Is that where
the dangerous elements bed down? Is this a biosphere
or a cannonball? In sunlight the strongest are suckling
their children (warm-blooded and cold-blooded evenly
spaced); and after the arterial tracks are laid down, only
well-wishers be advised to take to couch, though skipping
on lily pads not recommended
                              unless divorce from physics
original intention.

2/9: Lower East Side recombinant DNA

Custard crunchers vituperate, bialy manglers vindicate.
Doom-and-gloom discophiles waving styli at the fleeing
populace themselves tumble off the shores of a retracting
peninsula. *Whence peninsula you?* There's a camper full
of madrigals set to duplicate your spouse almost
halfway to the barbecue—uningestible you, indigestible
me. Circle back home towards the tonsured tension-spot,
only look what's ricocheting up the block. *Is that noise
in my head bothering you?* Whom am I supposed to give all
my quarters to? Grown men evaporating into the socks
of whacked-out pingpong tourists. The hapless *when,* which
regurgitates retroactively to the beginning of time,
commences to bounce conspiratorially from core of earth
to crust of moon, wherein detoxing cosmonaut whips up
a dip of cheese poems to God
                              with heavy chips of praise
to scramble the masses into Rutabaga Chintz.

2/10: Son of potty politics

Fear of the crimping tool, no phonecord in the hobbyhut
to tie shelter down, and a macabre *opus radius* in the kitchen
and bathroom to shock the living and the half-dead and the
would-bes *and* the wannabes. Which kinds of wiring might
bring opposing militias to consensus? Faulty towerbox
leans outward from a switching station: pulls cable taut,
acknowledges catcalls having sped fiber-optically continent
to continent, out through the phonecord and up the queen's
leotard, laying ions into adversaries unlike cloudbursts
of nickels slamming perfectly into coinslots until
parliament's in session. Only one finger of ten plucked
from the prime minister's love button way before anything
interesting happens. A sea of nail polish remover washing up
under the doormats of Hell, except this time there's a fire drill
and everyone's evacuated,
                              drunk on fructose
and incarcerated in toxic tofu.

2/11: And the women who love them

Beaming malaise preposterous, only keep your eyes in
the open position. Shoes propel you forward, hands'll try
(and tug you aside). Concrete path may cross the green,
but traverses will connect abruptly in your pantslegs.
Then cream creamery cheese, Lord; slumber in a mummy-
cloth of twill fatigues back-ordered from a reliquary
in advance of Year Zero. What time is it now, if only time
agrees not to be temporalized? Covered caravans lurch
into manifest, thrash in a brook of babbling testosterone
squeezing sperm-eggs from pebbles, at once rescheduling
wagon trains across the West to spiral into the tips
of their occupants' moccasins. Later on we get
spring and summer followed by autumn and winter;
piedmont into prairie, crater to Pacific, glandular accessories
before ancillary options;
                         a tricycle to peace
and a juggernaut to quiet.

2/12: How cop cars procreate

Plus plus [whatever else they did] plus plus. A hired hand
multiply related, limos and taxis in permanent photo-
tropic touch-bumperhood figuring fifty-one percent
for the ecclesiasts. Incidentally one might expect—having
dove down their straws and gushed deep into their milk-
shakes—exponent eject off the top and into the white
oblivion. Yet having only the more tremendous parts toted
aloft in a shoulder bag; noses out in front, built out
for the progeny via repeating acts of *crushing thy beercan
squarely upon thy forehead;* secondly via *slamming thy
John Thomas thrice against bedpost before somersaulting
into the sack.* Almost the last moments of Creationism
noted as freedom from reference beneath the endpapers
of the specialized bunko encyclopedia for dimwits,
now recorded for posterity
                              on the hairy palms of
That Was the Week That Was.

2/13: Defensive secretions

If not after all, after that. Owing the presence of headers
and the occasional sidewinder. Passing land, passing water:
"country" equals silence, and music the end-product following
systemic elimination. Passing wind, passing out: which
are you on? Where is the overlook and at which moment
do the delegating hysterics permit you to loosen your lips
and dribble down your bib? Cuss words and sex words and *yea*
though I laid a patch through the Valley of Death, I may as well
arm-fart Pig Latin for all this place bothers. Whatever I can put
into my mouth and expect self-propulsion a few hours
later, delusional retention only a little less strange
than a blowback from navel outward. So who cut the cheese?
Who's calling whom to task for what? As necrosis precipitates,
what should I make of all this? Meantime the cheese
keeps growing riper and riper,
                                        people and machines
ever disposed to gas us out of our houses.

2/14: Get out your spray paint

What do I want? I'm confused. Plant something in the garden
and pray for a toaster next spring, tracking the scent
off the map to a burned area out beyond the marginal(s).
Ears ring once before twisters cause appliances to waffle;
but who knows anything about it? The numbers, therefore,
have leapt into the crunch-box for to be thoroughly
simulated by the time Redeye Special hits the tunnel.
If there's a whim to be acted upon at which point becomes
it useless? Might produces impingement and everyone knows
how much more of it since last summer's riot. Blue-green
bronze patina ashtrays to sprout on tables never before
permitted in this neighborhood, now a fix of open-mouth
stupor straight into headlights and out through a brief-
case. Imagine allowing *these fucking yuppies* to strut across
my fucking pavement, observing

                            tick-tick-tick towards
infinity or sidewalk simulation thereof.

2/15: An old Hungarian adage

First to forget, first to coagulate. The Agronomist
of Human Souls got swallowed by his overseer's beeper
and conveyor'd down the incinerator chute. Tonight
they're serving Mass, but many teeth flew out at the moment
God bit them at the vertices of their wallets. There's this
saying, "a cow is a useful animal," but that was only after
a guy hung himself on a string of sausage. Will winter
arrive as a pendulum or a sofabed opening by itself
in the store? My guess the Other, which is another
manner of describing the sundry measurements these
incestuous bloodsuckers will soon commence to codify;
voluminous briefs puffing out from doorjambs, clogging up
dockets, shredded to ribbons and spooling around
the judge's chambers in obnoxious botanical frenzy,
while a planeload of acolytes,

                        stacked up in a fog
at the airport, crosses and examines considerably.

2/16: Dispositions, posthumously

Eyebrows of salvation past redemption to drink; best man
at the wicked wedding of the children revived to pasture.
Many stomps on the Pianist's fingers: call it a night,
meaning call out the murderous grasshoppers from green
canvas tent-city conjoined in a tarp—this what they'd have
to name Big Bastard Daylight after. Human turkey legs
wrenched off and juggled like bowling pins; lobster-claw
hands of the Healer sewing up eardrums so he could
beat on them some more, somewhere else. Only his mind
and no other which caused him to make mistakes, Culture
of Redress in paralytic due course. Nearly twelve billion
hands performing tasks and all, he's quite positive,
directed against him. But the repository of liquid waste
being smooth and obstacle-free, only a morning ejection
starts him on his way,
                    through dust and deliverance,
twisting down the drain.

III.

Indulgences on *I Trogloditi*

3/1: *Le droit du seigneur*

Feely-wiggly fingerpaint musses the flesh of succulent
Commie Nudists going to the bathroom incorrectly.
Squat where miasma-brokers stand, midway to the end
of humanity now that their dicks have been pickled
white and ferreted back to the ice chests. Many heads
be leveled until all of these and those dispense
their leach onto hexagonal oyster crackers in a bowl
of bubbling concrete sushi. If our most recent economic
bellwethers have any sizeable influence, the bells will
surely plummet; and in a lasting tribute to big teeth
and cellulite haunches, court is now in session. One bite
equals twenty-five rubs underneath, or else someone better
call the legislative body back from its recess and do
something quick. Am I repeating what you just chirped
into my head? Strike that,
                                what I meant was

Bird baby Bird.

3/2: The thing with the hillbilly nipples

Carnival cannibals reciprocate gracefully, occasionally
break into song. Where itineraries as such incapacitate
the scene, a rousing belch of success means the bile duct
looks after itself so long as it gets fed and massaged
at regular intervals. Which is nearly the way we like it,
but nobility was never a factor here. There's a palette
of sprockets rusting outside on the dock, half-erased
ideograms stenciled on the crates, except for this gunk
oozing out from the corners. These are the Wonder Gears
in case you're interested. The grand designations
of zest control and occipital defoliation. Monkey-
wrenching peat bogs of deliverance through shopping,
landed gentry laundry including some incredibly icky
undergarments and whatever else reeks. Only a few
spare fingers to nibble on
                          while waiting for dinner
to drive over.

3/3: Foodies will eat anything

What's the broth of broth? Incendiary? Allay it down
to the russet-kidneyed bowwow. And what of its lice?
Many kinds of unmistakable juices have seeped through
its gaskets and burned to a crust. But within an engine
a gravelly stomach runs on after shutoff, dieseling
some seconds off its life in the aggregate darkness,
itself in a holding pattern above evasive runways
connected to submersible terminals, all junctions
at traffic circles orbiting monuments to literary assholism,
my green discharge detonating clusters of giggling
bacteria, gossiping microbes so cute they ought to be
sculpted into lawn ornaments. As the wisdom of predatory
lendership so dictates, throw all your undesirables
into a pot and set the potatoes to boil. Then open
your eyes and see
        who's missing from the table.
(What table?)

3/4: Middle school megachurch

"Normative" was the Pez® word for "tomorrow" yesterday.
Groceries will fly into my apartment because my mother
told them to. There's a cleft in the Grand Unified Theory
of Maroon Polyester Sports Jackets and nothing to curtail
its progress to the opposite continent. In an open field of granular
foodstuffs the morning sun does not care to reflect. Only
the cashier's fingertips, atrophied due to pervasive use
of bar-code scanning, will point the way to the Parking Space
for Stay-At-Home-Dads. While at the other end of its butt-
crack, an unfortunate backyard extremity-grill metabolizes
down to critical mass; entire neighborhood digests itself;
exterminating angels get dispatched by Jesus from heaven
with orders to pump tissue-gas directly into life support,
as the first Vice President who opens the window
catches a load of etherous deposits

                                   from the mouth

of the smiling breathalyzer.

3/5: Book of Exodus cheat-sheet

Flagellation reminds me; disembowelment makes me forget.
What falls in between is the vaguest idea. On the seat
in my truck there's a baseball bat and a half-dozen
railroad spikes. Does this mean the termites are back?
This morning I set out to measure my variant thresholds
of tolerance and ended up kind of mutilating myself.
But something else gestures: a preponderance of pro-
tuberance bumping around in the rectums of creatures
thin-lipped and jiggly-assed, *mohair codpieces to the wind
from my lips to God's earplugs*—one possible definition
of a well-nutted meatloaf or a loudmouth-redneck-dusthead
interpretation of paradise on earth. This pleasant a life-
style takes time to coagulate. I've exactly ten minutes;
others have the rest of their lives to uncouple themselves
into smug satisfaction,
                              spotless voiding of their fluids
into the Public Sphinx.

3/6: Extra line breaks

Ergot taints the liquor crop / by letter I'm out the door /
in dreams I get punctured by marionettes / and then wrapped
in aluminum foil / for if lacy fungus mollify / what use
the badger shave / no softer brush was ever slaughtered
that greased the wheels of commerce, you two-timing
globalist horseprick! Grow extra digits in the roof
of your mouth / announce the redundancy-cure / blow
noxious fumes and retire to your dude ranch / if your animals
pass the frontier. Unluckily my friend *you've* been tagged
as a biohazard. Your children will be whisked away
and bred with famous monsters of filmland, or real ones
if the documents ever unravel. Alas, you were discovered
stripped to your boxers, fondling the manifolds off
your *rented* Pussy Magnet, milking the God of Intimacy thing.
Another five minutes of this
                                    and we are pulling
the plug.

3/7: Combustion theory

Motorheads sputter, woodheads splinter. Homegirl digs in
at flora with her weed-whacker, bearing sets of antennae
through the tops of her skulls. Twisting control knobs,
for example, from brain to machete happen at distance
from centers of power. Even a Beetle's got a master
cylinder stuck somewhere underneath; some also
stop with their brakes while others careen into fifth-
dimension outer space. But what's up with the Homeland?
What measures of Gestapitude have we to contend with
this year? Cream of humanity skimming off the shorelines
to indentured servitude job subordination. Do I hear
a motion to strike? Which plan the bastard supervisor will try
to implement according to the espionage of the planted
informant, divided as we are, standing under nostrils
of corruption and carried away
                              by phlegmatic jellyfish
straight out the exhaust.

3/8: The family that brays together

Too many jagged neurons, that's what makes it so:
spin the Magic Football to select your burial cloth
and theme music. Trees have been planted in memory
of your excellent backstroke as well as several minor
character flaws; but when they open you up to see
what killed you, don't expect the giggling fits
to abate. Those pterodactyls circling overhead are out
of their minds, and probably they'll just fall asleep
and crash down on top of us and that's what'll happen.
Those who say otherwise have regrettably now
become extinct—is there anything else on the agenda?
Last month I had big bubbles bursting inside my chest,
now they're floating around my head. If I go before you,
please don't forget to throw in a can of peroxide
every five hundred miles
                            or the hairdo will
seize on you.

3/9: Year of the ivory-billed ~~wood~~pecker

Fix my goddamn leaky roof or else. Cross public eloquence
with sacred contempt and soon the headlines close in
on you. Such episodes for example (your surname
conveniently mangled) owners of vast tracts of wastewater
frontage cry out for arousal of moonstruck peasants
and bleary-eyed deviationists, a program of intrigues
calmly sacked by its own ineptitude; moreover by world
cataclysm and the reconstruction of innumerable
embezzlements, acquaintances, honorable friends
and dispassionate engineers calling forth crystal-
spewing matrix displays. Kingdom of God splattering
indulgences on *i trogloditi* like Shit on a Shingle. Talking
tacos yammering about the weather while everywhere else
habitual hailstorms of cluster bombs merely upsetting
a few breakfasts. What do these
                            planet earth people
think? Something's dripping.

3/10: My kind of religion

Secret intelligence of the solar plexus: a mind straddling
molecular strings. In nature green waves, orthodoxy,
suppressive euphoria, censorious incomprehension
finally of its active organs of ridicule, but low
among priorities from the infrastructure's vantage.
Being relaxes beside itself, lapsing ingenuously
towards the problem. The physical world and its
complex of hospitals have devolved into the present;
but the situation is plastic and the body throws off
its fat; or the hospital sues itself for chronic nonpayment
and the mind forms a lesion in the bank. "Most confining,"
state the organs; "we concur," injects the bone.
Consider yourself a privileged bridesmaid the Controller
hasn't poisoned you; something you remember
having partially dissected
                    has been trickling
out your ears.

3/11: You again!

What's that hanging off your ass? Place checkmarks
beside each appropriate orifice, connect organ with function,
stand clear and see what transpires. If nothing then set
in the cellar to cure and forget about it. If something
take notes and post to this address: His Excellency Pope
Jaundiced Polyp II, 1600 Pennsylvania Avenue, Vatican
Township New Jersey; attention Cardinal Numbers. Send cash
or certified chits. Please crane your neck and observe
your hindquarters presently conferring with the insides
of your underpants; soon it will issue its response.
If low rumbling is heard take three steps backward;
if not, go outside and walk carefully to your car;
check pressure in left rear tire; if low do nothing
or reduce pressure in remaining three until flat,
then get behind
                    the wheel, lay back
and go to hell.

3/12: Free will is not enough?

The population's being difficult, here's mud in your eye.
We come from the planet of infantile table manners:
you've now got clearance to eject one pie. Last millennium
people threw up incessantly and so yielded bumper crops
to feed the starving masses, engorging themselves instead
on questionable animal by-products. Last century saw
etiquette books stuffed into secret lavatory receptacles,
pulped for recycling, rolled into cigarettes, flushed
to the sea. But only last weekend we discovered
everyone's down on all fours humping like their parents.
Better to obviate than motivate, what do they tender
to trample? A strange force in my hand wants to heave
something heavy in the direction of you, dear reader,
but my brain, stomach and asshole have conflicting opinions
on this. Unfortunately or fortunately

                                    the last word can wait
so long as we still have feet to vote with.

3/13: "Never again" again again again

Lick it, toe-sucker: you balloted that slime into office
so please *muzzle yer yap*. Here must one include oneself?
Let's postulate: how many [units] left until these Americans
wake up and smell their fusty armpits? I'll have a quarter
in dimes for every fingernail broken in ecstatic turning
of voting machine levers by enfranchising exurbanite crackers
refinancing their citizenship. Ring out the diplomats!
Ring in the smart bombs! Observe earnest shopkeepers
at victory parade beating up protesters: "go home scuzzball,"
"go home dirtbag." Get my commie faggot hindquarters
halfway the fuck uptown. Secondary new world order hands us
a tax break and commences firing. *My god I'm being
stabbed by my own dick!* What are the middle-middle up to?
(Hey bowel-face, they just poked your wife!) He's still in pajamas
on the sofa glued to his finger box.
                                    Will someone please
defenestrate this?

3/14: Inhuman resources

Widows sing of management shuffled; a turnpike ramp
curves across the bed. Morning shower shit and shave,
and here I am at work. Watch me throw up myself
onto your desktop, wondering why the soiled diapers
of your history of ideas are home soaking in the borax pail,
though it stinks far less than this cubicle. I didn't count
on barfing so much; you on the other hand will never
get your head out of the toilet. Bray at your terminal as you
administer your offspring; goose your secretary the way
you ogle your assets; beam your card-key to the other side
of the conference table and executives will make a miracle
with your pay stub. Elvis Christ, I'm starving with ecstasy.
If I require your assistance I'll click off the hook,
but for now move over and let me fade. If I ever regain
command of my faculties
                              I'll *get* my damn raise, they lie,
but not before they get whacked with the budget axe.

3/15: The mind of the electorate

Double-crush emasculator. *Man, that stuff just boils
my baloney off!* Members of the professions have appeared
on the farm: accountants at eight, auction at two,
foreclosure and dinner at six. Though come to think of it—
it what?—a smiley face having sprouted off the end of my
fuck finger, condensed into a globule spewing invective:
"glug glug" (end of recordable history); *"glug glug"* (my *bubbles*
are imploding); *"glug glug,"* (maybe I'll get my appendages back).
He's extremely happy; we're extremely unbelievably happy,
waving happy-happy branches and frantic-frantic digits.
And now that its legs will have commenced to animate,
a jump off the silo and into the abyss of their overalls;
what difference, if any, between hayseed and yahoo
only bull capital *B* and droppings lowercase *d* may
wholly survive to appreciate,
                                                though not this life
and excitedly away from the barbecue pit.

3/16: Pried from their cold dead hands

Bring you poker trousers *up;* calm before cough
and bark around the motorhome. The flags, the lawn,
miscellaneous tree trunks. He was born a maple
so the neighbors promptly tapped him for his sap,
boiled him down to sugar and shrubbery, *then* checked
what kind of hand he was holding. It's alive and pustular,
long threaded rods bulging under green felt tabletop
feeling limper as we speak. Meanwhile across the yard,
a pristine family soon to undergo the hissyfits
initiates a domino chain-spank, invoking irreality
and its collateral consequences. All persons present
rolling warm and caring souls over burst-open
bags of hospital refuse, gleaming hypos and fluid-
soaked gauze discharging into passersby, breaking
his concentration
                              and contributing to his
not having a nice day.

IV.

Rules of the Guest Culture

4/1: Break it up

Inside the vesicles of ordnance and supply, prisms
in a sanguineous spectrograph. Needles or needless,
which one is it? A groin kneed, a groin impeded; torn
tubule, sutured within, distresses its outline of sweet
meniscus to cauterize hemorrhaged tissue. Late faux-
antiquity bequeaths its colonies as irises data-map
to points of commotion. Love's mitochondria: hidden defect
of a solipsist's refuge, de-boned crania, broad-brimmed
penumbrae and interstitial benevolence. An amorality
of spigots. Eerie fantasia of the Vanishing Compañera
buffets the heart into daily rotation; yet given a slice
of bedroom paradox, a cinematic treatment abstains
its own closure—autistic as romance—or which lesson
might broker itself or its product, weighing in for inertia
on the Anvils of Mimesis,
                              tossed like a femur
to a Pile of the Living.

4/2: Mediation slam-dunks

Agree to stop pummeling one torso with another.
Force neighbors to pulverize kneecaps and teeth
stacked in a neighborly heap; such when I say "blow"
everyone suckle. Gravity pulling jackboots inward
spins as a halo or bowtie, spins as a cowbell or knot.
Atomizers atomize after one may have pressed
(button identity) reaction spreading radially outward
oozing from under arbor flesh; masticating biomass
until bedrock sparkles the periphery, until mud
coalesces to the walls, until lakebed mummifies
our now-commingled bodies, serpentine crack-pattern
blazing high desert countenance through the least
maligned orifice. Winks in the wild. To sully the "us"
in *pus*—a single contraction that refuses to settle for
angry feet of benevolence,
                              ceasing the dropkicks
to my lovely business up yours.

4/3: Exceptions to the blood feud

May we leave now? Rules of the Guest Culture: one
may not slice up one's enemy while nursing on his spouse.
Gratitude towards gimmickry is all *we've* been served
so *please remain shopping.* No requirement to people
the tables with barkers and card shills, expert counters
and the decoys assisting them. *Exorcist*-style rubber-
necking to spot-check the players with the big fuzzy dice
in their eyes; wheels of corporal punishment ear-boxed
by antsy flagellants. Automatic pity machines jackpot
regret with every hand thrown. And here's the instance:
we do not want to score we want to complete, soon
to be smacked into subtlety by convection or fission;
careering voices of the phantom consensus, rationalist
cheese wedges, manifold mobs distended with contentment
moving towards genocide
                              and other results-
oriented Acts of God.

4/4: Onward Christian solderers

This agreement stipulates to disgorge its agent. Receive
release then dismember to details, this year being
auspicious as forced opportunity allows us to buy off
the Rapture as spirits incline and desiccate. Representative
*Left Behind*edness, by this a providence and by this
a condition. We running exemptions as we running events
(read: we get to fail and/but we get to humiliate). Onto whom
will your ruminant alpha-pricks lactate? Neither bedded
in midtown nor splintered in the tunnel. We cannot sell
but neither can we rent and neither can we leave.
Speak to your portfolio, fertilize your mortgage, pimp
yourself to an eager grammarian. When autumn comes early
the love harvest's ruined; here the wasted convert
passes out in his buggy, the horse trotting its way
back to hearth and field
                              where the village awaits
with forgiveness and gut-clamps.

4/5: The view from Bushwick

Text insert. Who's the bastard here? Our landlord almost
pious in his negligence, he touches my rent the inspectors
will materialize. Surely the street concurs, but former
Dregs of Europe declass themselves relentlessly, doffing
their earphones and shoving them back in; this when
a neighborhood gives a big Hello Kitty punch in the face,
knocks them into the subway, PDA-wielding paramecia
pushing behind in the turnstile to bugger a free ride.
Young'uns stream out of their lofts and onto the platform;
this the Art Commute their realtors exhorted. Singular
acts of *kein*-ness: chatting each other to wireless torpor,
short-lease meditations on holy foreclosure; cleansed
conscience and an Oasis of Whitey slumming the *barrio*,
sexing up dollar shops, snorting tubs of take-out *pozole*
after under-tipping the Exploited
                              Delivery Amigo
who bikes it into their hands.

4/6: Socialism for runway models

Not a nosedive. Glossy and furrowed as a Teabagger's
Target. Here where the military tortures *in camera,*
sweet-toothed blood-striped anti-morning-gloried
erectile dysfunctionaires. *Them* pointed *there* banging
us over *here.* Exposure insensible as thong-ripping fingers,
meaning less like poetry and lesser as music; gauges
the latter's boundary, yet open to generate bulimic boy-
bandishness by us or the rest of homunculitude. Martial
legalities delivered by archangels be they liver-textured,
nefarious or sloughed. Cost-benefit intuited: neither
sphincter-diver nor uncapped flesh-vessel adorned
with predictable pallor, smug as an East Bloc émigré
essayist and his paeans to peasant musculature.
A series of rightward-leaning insta-books squeezes out
the pusscock end of publishing,

                                                    pursuant to advance
and serial rights perpetual.

4/7: Crepuscular observance

He is touching Himself, spread-eagled to a large cabbage
snowballing down the Via Dolorosa. Private observance
itches to publicize: out of the boardroom and straight
to the rape room. This period referred to as the Third Great
Awakening graduates to a comb-over, durable synthesis
of chemicals to captivate connubial kleptosophy as science
of manhandling. Vehicle semen, dick-deep in fuel cells
as hard-mouthed solution to the prom fuck problem,
glucose tolerant yet explodes like potassium, whirring
as a wastrel. Shopping Himself to Hisself, easy credit
mysticism buried in collection; sectarian footnotes
amiss as isn't what ain't and what ain't doesn't isn't.
You ain't isn't here. Age rightly wasted on the elderly;
their daily obsessions on their granddaughters' bosoms,
even as it pleaseth them
                                          to feel themselves up,
odd as they separate to slivers.

4/8: Flow control

Air-commode, waiting for you to douse me with something.
You've got belts, I'm a mess of steel plates. Permit us
to polarize, collapse into commerce; *yea, let projectiles*
plant their exceptional kisses, electoral Botox expressions
of Chlamydia; senators knocked-up squishy by constituents,
lobbies for ownership bliss. Blanket exhaust, surfeit of piety
strapped to its kayak, conjuring houses and condos and land,
leading to people and animals and your mother, undeserving
of those they clownishly molest with virtual personae
and weapons of crass induction. The evangelical correctness
of assembly given sweet pause to the flicking tongues
circling your aperture; gaping and ready glory-hole
opening and closing like a baby's mouth lip-synching
for its pacifier, dilating wide for the third biggest idea
that passes your palate, through your

                              system, out your ass

into the next person's mouth.

4/9: Dragonflies in the marinade

Mortify desire for the sake of our offspring. Over there
by the cannon a mediator takes notice: a human statue
cut to its boots, iced-over solid in mid-convolution, barely
aware of its ball-crushing handshake, gripping the airspace,
fondling its weeds, falling rump-first into negotiated settlement
like a teen into his clergyman's Johnson. Digressing
to desire when generally convenient; he an exemplar
of proof and figure, considering calculation or duplicitous
immersion as he seizes his organ to inspect himself.
Only love that escapes his storyline's meddling: secreting
fumes onto money and its opposite, prayer into nightmares
of smoldering hamlets, if by that he means all matter
positioned beyond his own skin; winding his conscience
into a shriek loud enough to be heard by the Godling
to which his aging parents elicit
                              from their gurneys,
wheeling from Death Class home.

4/10: Booby traps

Shut it down, figure it out or wither in place. Weep
if groveling then breathe on it lest one amuse oneself
in an orgy of green succulence. The body from without:
entertains to astonish without devolving to facts,
or lowering one's baggage into the River of Shrinkage.
An empathy for syllables travels the nerves from titty
to toenail, kneaded like scrota yet resembling value
found only played off transactions; a cartoon epiphany
late for its love fest, barking tips to triumphalists armed
to the armpits with Uvulae of Ridicule. *Velvet hammer*
blunted trauma: slovenly ovine pulchritude enjoined
to ambition—as if the pain bending deep into your back
were unimpressed with its carping. You being dragged
across knee-rubbing concrete, chest restrained
and staring at your
                    handler's chopper
as it hovers over breakfast.

4/11: Better than cable

Particles escape and your books are overdue. Billionaire
Space Tourist gets date-raped on the Shuttle, stunned
as his contract disallows recourse. In the orbiting scrubbers,
CO_2 dust-mites nod their assent; their pee filters oxygen
pushed through a HEPA bag, creatures imprisoned secure
down below. Noodle-strokers? *Poodle-pokers!* Each assigned
an obscure constellation, zipping about the cargo bay
in a mutually festive mercy-fuck. Swimming in primo alkaloids,
seven tiny minks on board convene to cook up vendettas.
Agitated astronauts kick 'em like hacky sacks, bounce
their pelts off structural braces, daydreaming zero-G
nuptials with mediocre DJs and bridal veils assembled
from available scalps—same as how it happens back home
in the Garment Zone—there but for the grace of NASA
go they, furriers in spacesuits,
                            tongues quick-frozen
to the satellite dish.

4/12: Better than phone sex

Three and thrust. If they open our bellies they'll find it
there quivering, mercifully blackened, nicely toned
from skin to viscera. Frantic scraping at one's innards
like polenta from a saucepan, this how professional
onlookers eulogize, only they get paid in full up front.
Toggle the tear ducts—*ka-ching*—psychic flatulence
cascades through the parlors; you chasing wished-for
extensions of your gene pool, sullen replication
of breath between spasms, nausea mornings
and absolute void. Functionally pregnant: solemn promise
of entombment in mayonnaise, suspension stirred
by retractable fingers. Love screeds sewn into flesh;
tasks that exhaust your spiritual capital and hence
producing expected results, all in service of evading
the billowing bedsheets
                    defining the volume
of our eyes and lips reflected/refracted/redacted.

4/13: Here kitty kitty

Pets expire in moonlit caskets. *Your nuts wouldn't*
clog up a thimble. When men begin to convocate,
better to blast before they fry up your relatives
as giant cocks batter the landscape, split open
like milkweed and spore off divisions of airborne
cocklets. So who's thatching *scenery* to the roofs
of their cottages? Elevated windows floating over
the naked millions rioting silently in their boxcars;
enormous handfuls of seed corn scattered upland
to sow the pubis crop for next season's pill-popping
prayer breakfasts. Claustrophobic wedding socials
organized around doorways with freeze-dried felines
piled in pyramids near the fire exits. Housecats gone
to heaven as *un*just reward for lifetimes of arrogance,
only to discover canine angels
                                        managing the line,
wagging their blood-chunks behind them.

4/14: These are the cries of the turnips

Crack of desire, why are they killing the quiet ones?
Let them train their lethal frequencies on themselves
and their invisible playmates. We couldn't levitate
a calf liver without a nice evening's wanker, so please
give the kettles a good clang with a pipe wrench.
Roust the slumbering arts administrators, cataleptic
after decades of making beds for others to fuck in. Give us
a large grant for me not to execute my suicide-bomb
theater piece. Our dancers have been shackled securely
to the storm drains, musicians duct-taped beneath them.
Now our ears are full of love letters from creditors
and hate mail from actors, watching each body movement
webcammed from offshore IP addresses, their overworked
interns soldered to desks, hands on their crotches, making
prose out of remittance codes

                              hoping their gods won't
catch them *ex flagrante.*

4/15: Underwater money

Ink pools into aneurysms; *too bad your laptop won't*
give you a love-job. Half-staring at the cuttlefish
floating in the aquarium, lazily spewing out dark
cocktail urine, releasing their sex tentacles to droop
down beneath, pulsing their coinage between them.
Celebratory discharge: what are they doing and what
am I obligated to do for them? A nastiness threshold
for digital communicants, but not for cuttlefish. Marine
movements recorded ironically: undersea arteries
weakened and ballooning. Cynical death cherubs
watching their watches "ticking" onscreen—nominally
elsewhere—to squat up a server six time zones away,
tabulate mollusks and market their cartilage, blow
excretion deposits and blacken the bank accounts
of oven-fried hipsters, the ones
                              typing pre-absolved
penance on keypads tattooed on their *culos.*

4/16: Chow time

Engage. At penult the star-body commences expansion,
values even the dead might learn. Memory insufficient
to peel enough feeling from jellied cadavers in repose
on acid-etched porcelain tomb plaques. A line of heads
apple-in-mouth, burping glass-eyed acknowledgement
to their well-swaddled spirits. So cornered in this regard,
how do they rectify their cells? In what do they wash
their public misgivings? Why are they squandering
their allotted face time? Precious gift of compromised
pleasure? Resurrection amenable to performative drill-downs,
organ donors *livid!* Charley-horsed thighs limp down
the hallways of down-market mortuaries, sending themselves
to the dustiest boneyard whose iron perimeters encase
their graves to keep the rest of us out; a great supine mass
in their vaults gazing skyward,
                                    preening themselves
to feed on the next ones.

ROOF BOOKS

the best in language since 1976

Recent Titles

- Guest, Barbara. **Dürer in the Window, Reflexions on Art**.
  Book design by Richard Tuttle. Four color throughout. 80p. $24.95.
- Perelman, Bob. **Iflife**. 140p. $13.95.
- Arakawa, Gins, Madeline. **Making Dying Illegal**. 224p. $22.95.
- Stefans, Brian Kim. **Kluge**. 128p. $13.95
- Gordon, Nada. **Folly**. 128p. $13.95
- Shaw, Lytle, editor. **Nineteen Lines: A Drawing Center Writing Anthology**. 336p. $24.95

ROOF BOOKS are published by
Segue Foundation • 300 Bowery • New York, NY 10012
Visit our website at **seguefoundation.com**

ROOF BOOKS are distributed by
SMALL PRESS DISTRIBUTION
1341 Seventh Avenue • Berkeley, CA. 94710-1403.
Phone orders: 800-869-7553
spdbooks.org